The European Union

Political, Social, and Economic Cooperation

The
EUROPEAN UNION

POLITICAL, SOCIAL, AND ECONOMIC COOPERATION

The European Union

Political, Social, and Economic Cooperation

LITHUANIA

by
Heather Docalavich

Mason Crest Publishers
Philadelphia

Mason Crest Publishers Inc.
370 Reed Road, Broomall, Pennsylvania 19008
(866) MCP-BOOK (toll free)
www.masoncrest.com

First printing
1 2 3 4 5 6 7 8 9 10

Library of Congress Cataloging-in-Publication Data

Docalavich, Heather.
    Lithuania / by Heather Docalavich.
        p. cm. — (The European Union)
    Includes index.
    ISBN 1-4222-0054-X
    ISBN 1-4222-0038-8 (series)
1. Lithuania—Juvenile literature. 2. European Union–Lithuania—Juvenile literature. I. Title. II. Series:
European Union (Series) (Philadelphia, Pa.)
    DK505.23.D63 2006
    947.93—dc22
                                    2005018343

Produced by Harding House Publishing Service, Inc.
www.hardinghousepages.com
Interior design by Benjamin Stewart.
Cover design by MK Bassett-Harvey
Printed in the Hashemite Kingdom of Jordan.

CONTENTS

THE EUROPEAN UNION

GREENLAND SEA

ICELAND
Reykjavik

BARENTS SEA

NORWEGIAN SEA

FINLAND
Tampere

NORWAY
Trondheim
Bergen
Lillehammer
Oslo
Kristiansand

Turku
Helsinki

RUSSIA

Moscow

SWEDEN
Stockholm
Norrköping
Gothenburg

ESTONIA
Tallinn
Tartu

Gulf of Finland

DENMARK
Aalborg
Odense
Helsingborg
Malmö
Copenhagen

LATVIA
Ventspils
Liepāja
Riga
Daugavpils

LITHUANIA
Klaipėda
Kaunas
Vilnius

BALTIC SEA

Gulf of Bothnia

Gulf of Riga

White Sea

GLASGOW Edinburgh
UNITED KINGDOM
Belfast
IRELAND
Dublin
Killarney
Cork
Liverpool
Manchester
Birmingham
London

NORTH SEA

RUSSIA
Gdansk

BELARUS
Minsk

POLAND
Warsaw

Irish Sea
St. George's Channel

THE NETHERLANDS
The Hague
Rotterdam
Amsterdam
BELGIUM
Brussels
LUXEMBOURG
Luxembourg
Paris

Hamburg
Berlin
Düsseldorf
Cologne
GERMANY
Frankfurt Main
Leipzig
Dresden
Stuttgart

Wroclaw
Kraków
CZECH REPUBLIC
Plzeň
Prague
Brno
Košice
SLOVAKIA

UKRAINE
Kyiv

English Channel

FRANCE
Nantes
Bordeaux
Lyons

Munich
Linz
Salzburg
Vienna
Bratislava
AUSTRIA
Bern
SWITZERLAND
HUNGARY
Győr
Budapest
Szeged

MOLDOVA
Chisinau

ROMANIA
Bucharest

Sea of Azov

Toulouse
Marseille
Nice
Genoa
Turin
Milan
Venice
Trieste
Ljubljana
Zagreb
SLOVENIA
BOSNIA-HERCEGOVINA
CROATIA
Sarajevo
Belgrade
YUGOSLAVIA

Sofia
BULGARIA

BLACK SEA

Bay of Biscay

PORTUGAL
Porto
Lisbon
Faro
Vigo
Bilbao
Madrid
Barcelona
Valencia
Seville

SPAIN

Florence
ITALY
Rome
Naples

ADRIATIC SEA

TYRRHENIAN SEA

Skopje
MACEDONIA
Tirana
ALBANIA
Thessaloniki

Ankara

TURKEY

AEGEAN SEA

IONIAN SEA

GREECE
Athens
Kalamata

Sea of Crete

CYPRUS
Lefkosia (Nicosia)
Lemesos

SYRIA

LEBANON
Damascus

MEDITERRANEAN SEA

Strait of Gibraltar

Gulf of Lion

MALTA
Valetta

Rabat
Algiers
MOROCCO
ALGERIA
Tunis
TUNISIA
Tripoli
LIBYA

MEDITERRANEAN SEA

Cairo

ISRAEL & THE PALESTINIAN TERRITORIES
Amman
JORDAN

EGYPT

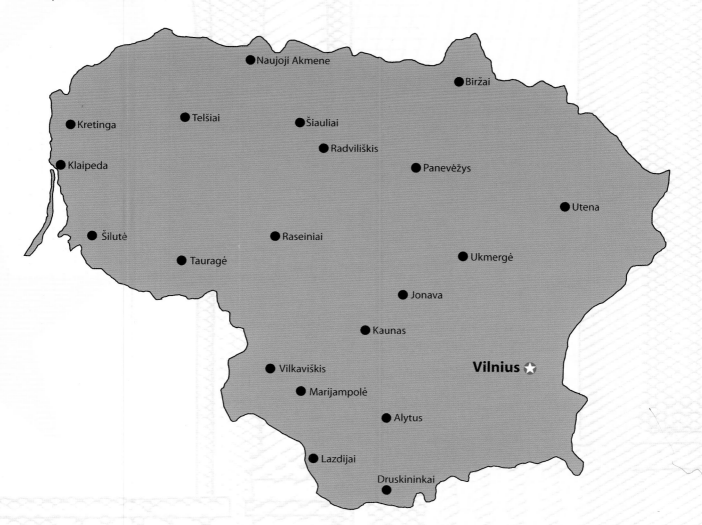

LITHUANIA

European Union Member since 2004

- Naujoji Akmene
- Biržai
- Kretinga
- Telšiai
- Šiauliai
- Radviliškis
- Klaipeda
- Panevėžys
- Utena
- Šilutė
- Raseiniai
- Ukmergė
- Tauragė
- Jonava
- Kaunas
- **Vilnius** ☆
- Vilkaviškis
- Marijampolė
- Alytus
- Lazdijai
- Druskininkai

INTRODUCTION

Sixty years ago, Europe lay scarred from the battles of the Second World War. During the next several years, a plan began to take shape that would unite the countries of the European continent so that future wars would be inconceivable. On May 9, 1950, French Foreign Minister Robert Schuman issued a declaration calling on France, Germany, and other European countries to pool together their coal and steel production as "the first concrete foundation of a European federation." "Europe Day" is celebrated each year on May 9 to commemorate the beginning of the European Union (EU).

The EU consists of twenty-five countries, spanning the continent from Ireland in the west to the border of Russia in the east. Eight of the ten most recently admitted EU member states are former communist regimes that were behind the Iron Curtain for most of the latter half of the twentieth century.

Any European country with a democratic government, a functioning market economy, respect for fundamental rights, and a government capable of implementing EU laws and policies may apply for membership. Bulgaria and Romania are set to join the EU in 2007. Croatia and Turkey have also embarked on the road to EU membership.

While the EU began as an idea to ensure peace in Europe through interconnected economies, it has evolved into so much more today:

- Citizens can travel freely throughout most of the EU without carrying a passport and without stopping for border checks.

- EU citizens can live, work, study, and retire in another EU country if they wish.

- The euro, the single currency accepted throughout twelve of the EU countries (with more to come), is one of the EU's most tangible achievements, facilitating commerce and making possible a single financial market that benefits both individuals and businesses.

- The EU ensures cooperation in the fight against cross-border crime and terrorism.

- The EU is spearheading world efforts to preserve the environment.

- As the world's largest trading bloc, the EU uses its influence to promote fair rules for world trade, ensuring that globalization also benefits the poorest countries.

- The EU is already the world's largest donor of humanitarian aid and development assistance, providing 55 percent of global official development assistance to developing countries in 2004.

The EU is neither a nation intended to replace existing nations, nor an international organization. The EU is unique—its member countries have established common institutions to which they delegate some of their sovereignty so that decisions on matters of joint interest can be made democratically at the European level.

Europe is a continent with many different traditions and languages, but with shared values such as democracy, freedom, and social justice, cherished values well known to North Americans. Indeed, the EU motto is "United in Diversity."

Enjoy your reading. Take advantage of this chance to learn more about Europe and the EU!

Ambassador John Bruton,
Head of Delegation of the European Commission, Washington, D.C.

The Lithuanian landscape is dotted with numerous ponds and lakes.

CHAPTER 1

THE LANDSCAPE

Welcome to Lithuania! Situated on the eastern shore of the Baltic Sea, Lithuania covers an area of about 40,513 square miles (65,200 sq. kilometers). About the size of West Virginia, it is larger in area than the more populous nations of Belgium, Denmark, the Netherlands, or Switzerland. The largest of the three Baltic States, Lithuania is bordered by Latvia to the north, Belarus to the southeast, Poland to the south, and the Kaliningrad Region of Russia to the southwest. The nearly landlocked nation has 67 miles (108 kilometers) of Baltic seashore. The Baltic coast offers sandy beaches and pine forests that attract thousands of tourists every year.

PLAINS, HIGHLANDS, AND SEASHORES

Lithuania lies at the edge of the East European Plain. The geographic features seen in Lithuania today are the result of glacial activity that occurred long ago in the region's prehistoric past. A rolling, low-lying plain comprises most of the central area of the country. This fertile plain with its gently rolling hills was formed as ancient glaciers pushed up mounds of soil and debris. The plain separates the eastern and western highlands of the country. These uplands, once heavily forested, are also the result of prehistoric glacial activity. The nation's highest point, Juozapines Hill, is located in the east, near the capital city of Vilnius. Its elevation reaches 965 feet (294 meters) above sea level.

The shores of the Baltic Sea provide sandy beaches for recreation and important access for transport and shipping. A sandbar, called the Curonian Spit, about 62 miles (100 kilometers) long and 2.5 miles (less than 4 kilometers) wide shelters more than half of the coast. Thanks to recent environmental legislation, much of that area is now a national park. The water between the sandbar and the mainland is called the Curonian Lagoon. Amber, sometimes referred to as Lithuanian gold, frequently washes up onto the Curonian Spit. Formed from the resin of ancient pine trees that lived millions of years ago, over time, the amber hardened into golden or red translucent deposits, some of which contain prehistoric insects that were trapped in the resin as it hardened. Today, amber is used to make jewelry and is a valuable export.

RIVERS AND LAKES

The Lithuanian landscape is punctuated by 2,833 lakes and an additional 1,600 ponds. The majority of the lakes are found in the eastern part of the

The rolling plain of central Lithuania is well watered and possesses many rivers and streams.

In ancient Lithuania, much of the land was forested but over the years farmers have cleared much of the land to raise crops.

country. Lithuania also has 758 rivers. The largest river is the Nemunas, with a total length of 570 miles (917 kilometers), which originates in neighboring Belarus. The other larger waterways are the Neris, the Venta, and Sesupe rivers. However, only 373 miles (600 kilometers) of Lithuania's rivers are **navigable**.

A TEMPERATE CLIMATE

Lithuania's climate is temperate, and days are generally mild but cool. The eastern regions are usually colder than the area along the coast. In winter, between November and March, the temperature may fall to 14°F (–10°C) or lower, and much of the country is covered with snow. In summer, the temperature may reach a high of 71.6°F (22°C), and it often rains. Average annual precipitation is 28.22 inches (717 millimeters) on the coast and 19.29 inches (490 millimeters) in the eastern part of the country. The growing season lasts for about two hundred days each year, providing a hospitable environment for many kinds of agriculture.

Trees, Plants, and Wildlife

At one time, thick forests covered much of the land, but over the years, farmers have cleared the land for crops. Today, woodlands cover only one-quarter of Lithuania. Pine trees grow along the coast and in the south, while oak trees are more commonly found in the central region. Lithuanian forests play an important part in the nation's culture and folk tales. During times of war, the forests were a haven for those in danger. The oak tree was worshipped during **pagan** times and today represents longevity and strength. Even in modern times, Lithuanians still plant oak trees to mark important occasions.

Edible plants such as mushrooms, wild strawberries, cranberries, raspberries, and bilberries grow in the southern pine forests. Lithuania's nature reserves and national parks provide a refuge for a wide variety of wildlife, including elk, deer, wolves, foxes, and wild boar. Bird species include white storks, herons, geese, ducks, swans, eagles, and hawks.

Environmental Concerns

Lithuania has worked diligently to improve its environmental health, which was seriously neglected over much of the last century. A host of environmental problems still exist, although major efforts have been made to bring environmental standards in line with those of the other nations of Europe who are Lithuania's partners in the European Union (EU).

The country's **flora** and **fauna** have suffered from heavy drainage of land for agricultural use. Environmental problems of a different nature were created by the development of environmentally unsafe industries, including the Ignalina nuclear power plant, which still operates two aging nuclear reactors, and a host of factories that pollute the air and empty dangerous waste into rivers and lakes. According to calculations by experts, nearly one-third of Lithuanian territory is covered by polluted air at any given time.

To help preserve the small areas that have not suffered from environmental damage, the Lithuanian government has made sweeping environmental reforms and invested in developing a national system of parks and preserves to help protect its remaining natural treasures. There are five national parks in Lithuania and several nature reserves, the highlight being the Kursiu Nerija National Park, which preserves a unique coastal habitat made up of high dunes, pine forests, sandy beaches, lagoons, and tidal flats.

The Lithuanian capital of Vilnius is beautiful, historic, and a popular spot for revelers in the evening.

2 Lithuania's History and Government

Lithuania has not always existed as the country it is today. For centuries, the area was subject to invasion and domination by larger, more powerful nations, and this reality has defined the destiny of Lithuania and its people. Having emerged as a newly independent state in 1990, Lithuania is now a united, democratic country, a member of the United Nations, and a new member of the EU. As a nation, Lithuania is committed to peace and building good relations with other countries.

ANCIENT LITHUANIA

Lithuania belongs to the Baltic group of nations. Their ancestors, the ancient Balts, moved to the region about 3000 BCE from beyond the Volga

ally peace-loving **agrarian** societies. The Couronians, on the west coast of the Baltic Sea, were a warlike society who sustained themselves through the periodic invasion and looting of other tribes. They became known as the "Vikings of the Baltic." The Latgallians, later known as Latvians, developed a fairly sophisticated society based on commerce and trade. The Prussians were conquered by the Teutonic Knights, and, ironically, the name "Prussia" was taken over by the Germanic conquerors who destroyed or **assimilated** Prussia's original, Slavic inhabitants. Other groups also died out or were assimilated by their neighbors. Only the cultures of the Lithuanians and the Latvians have survived to modern times.

DATING SYSTEMS AND THEIR MEANING

You might be accustomed to seeing dates expressed with the abbreviations BC or AD, as in the year 1000 BC or the year AD 1900. For centuries, this dating system has been the most common in the Western world. However, since BC and AD are based on Christianity (BC stands for Before Christ and AD stands for *anno Domini*, Latin for "in the year of our Lord"), many people now prefer to use abbreviations that people from all religions can be comfortable using. The abbreviations BCE (meaning Before Common Era) and CE (meaning Common Era) mark time in the same way (for example, 1000 BC is the same year as 1000 BCE, and AD 1900 is the same year as 1900 CE), but BCE and CE do not have the same religious overtones as BC and AD.

River in central Russia. Over time, the flourishing trade of Baltic amber with Rome drew new settlers from other areas of Europe. Between 900 and 1000 CE, the inhabitants of the area were divided into different language groups: Lithuanians, Prussians, Selonians, Semgallians, Couronians, and Latgallians.

The farming cultures of the Selonians and Semgallians, the smallest groups, were gener-

LITHUANIAN STATEHOOD AND THE POLISH LITHUANIAN COMMONWEALTH

The origins of the Lithuanian **nation-state** date from the early Middle Ages. Lithuania first emerged as a nation in 1230 under the leadership of a ruler named Mindaugas. He united Lithuanian tribes to defend against attacks by the Teutonic Knights, who had conquered the tribes of Prussia and also parts of present-day Latvia. The Teutonic Knights were a group of Germanic Christians whose goal was to conquer the Baltic territories in order to convert its people to Christianity.

In an effort to make peace, Mindaugas converted to Roman Catholicism in 1251, and in 1253, he became king. Unfortunately, the local nobility disagreed with his policy of coexistence with the Teutonic Knights and his desire for commerce with Western Europe. Mindaugas was

The old Lithuanian capital of Trakai possesses two lakeside castles set in a large national park.

killed, the monarchy was lost, and the country reverted to paganism. His successors sought expansion and trade in the Slavic nations to the east.

By the end of the fourteenth century, Lithuania had grown powerful and ruled large expanses of land to the east, including modern-day Belarus and parts of the Ukraine. Under increasing military pressure from Germany, Grand Duke Jagiello, Lithuania's ruler, faced a dilemma. When Lithuania could no longer stand alone, should he look to the East or the West for political and military alliances?

Jagiello chose to open links to Western Europe as a means to defeat the Germans, who claimed that their mission was not to conquer the Lithuanians but to **Catholicize** them. He was offered the crown of Poland, which he accepted in

Many districts of Vilnius possess housing that has not substantially improved for decades.

1386. In return for the crown, Jagiello promised to convert all of Lithuania to Roman Catholicism. Lithuania was the last predominantly pagan country in Europe to convert. The newly allied forces of Poland and Lithuania then defeated the Germans in the Battle of Tannenberg in 1410, ending all Germanic expansion to the east.

In 1569, Lithuania and Poland united into a single state, the Polish-Lithuanian Commonwealth, whose capital was Krakow. During this period, the Polish nobility and the Roman Catholic Church dominated Lithuania's political life, resulting in neglect of the Lithuanian language and introduction of Polish cultural and political institutions. It also resulted in the adoption of Western models of education. For 226 years, Lithuania was tied to Poland and its destiny.

RUSSIAN RULE

By the 1700s, Russia had begun to set its sights on expansion in hopes of securing a clear passage to Western Europe. By 1795, a series of military victories and an alliance between the Germanic states of Prussia and Austria with the Russian Empire ended the independent existence of the Polish-Lithuanian Commonwealth. Lithuania became a province of **czarist** Russia. Rebellions in 1831 and 1863 failed to liberate the country. The Russian Empire began to systematically eliminate Polish influence on Lithuania and introduced Russian law, language, and religion. Under czarist rule, Lithuanian schools were forbidden, Lithuanian publications in the Latin script were outlawed, and the activities of the Roman Catholic Church were severely restricted.

The dawn of the nineteenth century marked a period of national awakening across Europe. The aggression of the French general, Napoleon Bonaparte, created a wave of **nationalism** that swept across the continent. The concept of a nation as a group of people linked by a common language and culture had great appeal to the Lithuanian people who were chafing under foreign rule. Inspired by the renewed interest in national identity that was taking place among their neighbors to the west, the Lithuanian intellectual **elite** soon launched a national revival of their own.

Initial national movements were limited to discussions of language, literature, and culture. However, soon the nationalists were no longer content with cultural and social reform but had set their sights on political change. An independent and democratic Lithuania was the goal of these early **activists**, but it would take several more years before their hopes could be realized.

WORLD WAR I AND INDEPENDENCE

The growing Lithuanian nationalist movement eventually produced demands for self-government. In 1905, Lithuania became the first Russian province to demand its freedom. Independence was not achieved, however, because the czar firmly reestablished his rule after a failed revolution in 1905. Nevertheless, the dream of an independent Lithuania was not abandoned.

Meanwhile, the inability of European leaders to ease political tensions between the different nationalities under their rule eventually led to war. World War I began on June 28, 1914, when Gavrilo Princip, a Serbian nationalist, assassinated Austrian archduke Franz Ferdinand and his wife, Sophie. Russia allied with Serbia. Germany sided with Austria and soon declared war on Russia. After France declared its support for Russia, Germany attacked France. German troops then invaded Belgium, a **neutral** country that stood between German forces and Paris. Great Britain declared war on Germany.

When the war came to a close, Lithuanian nationalists saw their opportunity in the confusion that followed. As borders began to be redrawn all across Europe, the collapse of the two great European empires, Russia and Germany, made it possible for Lithuania to assert its **statehood**. Germany's attempt to persuade Lithuania to become a German **protectorate** was unsuccessful. On February 16, 1918, Lithuania declared its complete independence, and modern Lithuania still celebrates that day as its Independence Day.

A series of military conflicts immediately followed Lithuania's declaration of independence. Between 1918 and 1920, Lithuania successfully fought a war against the newly independent Poland to defend its **sovereignty**. At the end of 1920, however, Poland **annexed** Lithuania's capital city of Vilnius. This ended all diplomatic ties between Lithuania and Poland. After declaring its independence, Lithuania also fought against the Bermondt-Avalov army, a German-sponsored group of military **opportunists** who sought to take advantage of the **power vacuum** in the region and establish German control over the Baltic States, and against the Red Army of the newly formed Soviet Union. On July 9, 1920, Soviet leader Vladimir Lenin signed a peace treaty with Lithuania, forever renouncing Russia's claims to the territory and officially recognizing the Lithuanian state.

In the early 1920s, Lithuania also had a border dispute with Germany. The city and region of Klaipeda had been under German rule for the previous seven hundred years. Primarily inhabited by Lithuanians, it was separated from Germany following World War I and placed under French control. In 1923, Lithuanians organized a revolt and took over the Klaipeda region.

This series of conflicts and crises caused problems in Lithuania's international diplomacy. The democratic government was perceived as unstable by foreign observers, who predicted that the country's independence would be short lived. Internally, however, each political and military success fed the development of a new Lithuanian national identity and cultural awareness, leading to the decline of German and Polish cultural influences.

Lithuania's early disorganization and its constant conflicts with other powers in the region caused a delay in its official recognition by the

The practice of Catholicism was effectively discouraged by the Communist rulers of Lithuania, but Catholic buildings now are being restored throughout the capital of Vilnius.

major Western powers. In 1922, the United States became the last country to do so. Independent Lithuania, led by youthful and energetic politicians mostly in their thirties or early forties, became a thriving democratic republic. However, this government lacked the strong backing of the general population (as many as one-third of who were illiterate and unfamiliar with democratic practices) or the military. In 1926, the **coalition government** was removed by a military **coup**. Antanas Smetona, a former president, eventually established an **authoritarian** government. All opposition political parties were outlawed and the press **censored**, but Smetona did not completely rescind individual civil rights.

Despite the loss of a representative government, Lithuania made great strides in nation building and development during this period. A **progressive** land reform program was introduced in 1922, and economic reforms helped to build a thriving economy. The nation's first universities were established (there had been no institutions of higher education and very few secondary schools under Russian rule), and the public education system was expanded. As a result, illiteracy was greatly reduced. Even though an authoritarian dictator controlled Lithuania, in many ways the nation was experiencing a degree of personal freedom impossible under Russian rule. This fueled an explosion in the fields of art and literature. Lithuanian artists and writers of the period produced works that have become classics.

WORLD WAR II AND THE END OF INDEPENDENCE

By 1933, Adolf Hitler had come to power in Germany, and by 1938, he had occupied neighboring Austria. His stated objective was to unify all ethnic German peoples. He soon demanded the surrender of Czechoslovakia's Sudetenland, taking up the cause of the Sudeten Germans. On September 29, 1938, France, Germany, Italy, and Great Britain signed the Munich Agreement, demanding that Czechoslovakia surrender the Sudetenland to Germany in exchange for a promise of peace. However, in March 1939, Hitler went back on his agreement and invaded the remainder of Czechoslovakia; this action was followed by an invasion of Poland. Well aware of Hitler's ambitious plans to conquer Europe, Soviet leader Josef Stalin negotiated the secret Molotov-Ribbentrop Pact. This agreement pledged that Nazi Germany would not attack the Soviet Union, and in return, the Soviets would not oppose further Nazi expansion.

This pact changed the value of the Baltic States overnight. Lithuania had now become an area of strategic interest to the USSR. In October 1939, the Soviet Union forced a treaty on Lithuania that allowed Moscow to move 20,000 troops into the country. In return, the city of Vilnius, now also occupied by Soviet troops, was granted to

Lithuania's recent history is darkened by the massacres of Jews that occurred in the country during World War II. These walls were part of a concentration camp located on the outskirts of Kaunas.

Lithuania. On June 15, 1940, Lithuania was over-run by the Red Army. The communists quickly installed a **puppet government**. Once installed, the new communist government request-ed membership in the Soviet Union, against the wishes of the majority of the people. A takeover of this magnitude could not be accomplished without some form of opposition, so to eliminate dissent, the Soviets ordered the **deportation** of thou-sands of Lithuanians to Siberia. An estimated 30,000 people were deported in the middle of the night on June 14, 1941.

This large Soviet-era monument marks the area where more than 50,000 people were killed by Nazis outside the central city of Kaunas.

As World War II progressed, Lithuania was occupied by Nazi forces. During this time, more than 85 percent of the nation's Jews were murdered in concentration camps or by Nazi death squads. An anti-Nazi resistance movement soon formed, publishing underground newspapers, organizing economic boycotts, and gathering arms. The Nazis responded by arresting Lithuanian nationalists and by closing universities. Many tens of thousands of people were deported to work in Germany and perished in prisons or concentration camps. Both the Russians and the Germans conscripted Lithuanian men for forced service in the army, causing devastating losses

among a population with no real loyalty to either side.

By 1944, the Soviet armies had recaptured Lithuania, although Klaipeda did not fall until January 1945. However, Lithuania's full domination by Soviet forces was obstructed from 1944 to 1952 by a **guerrilla** resistance movement, which cost an estimated 20,000 to 30,000 Lithuanian casualties. As a means to restore order and promote a "collective" mindset among the populace, the Soviets began an intensive program of **Russification**.

COMMUNIST RULE

The years immediately following World War II are still remembered as a time of great trouble for the Lithuanian people. Many changes were forced on the Lithuanian people to assimilate them into the Russian-dominated culture of the Soviet Union. All government activity, including education, was now to be conducted in Russian. Any Lithuanians suspected of having anti-Soviet political beliefs were imprisoned or deported to Siberia. All private ownership of land and industry was outlawed. Communists seized all private property and transferred ownership to the state. The Roman Catholic Church was severely persecuted, one bishop was shot, and a number of other influential clergymen were imprisoned or deported. Many Lithuanians who had the means to do so fled to democratic countries in the West.

As a movement, organized resistance was first inspired by efforts to defend the Roman Catholic Church. After the Soviets invaded Czechoslovakia in 1968, repression increased throughout the Soviet Union, and the resistance movement spread. In the 1970s, Lithuania had numerous illegal, anticommunist publications. In 1972, a young student, Romas Kalanta, **immolated** himself in protest against Soviet rule. A street rebellion followed, as Lithuanian students raged against the injustices of communist oppression. The Soviet Army was called in to end the riot, and a number of students were killed or imprisoned.

A RENEWED CRY FOR INDEPENDENCE

Despite the efforts of the underground resistance, Soviet control of Lithuania went largely unchallenged for many decades, in part due to the harsh penalties imposed for dissent. The lasting power of communist rule was also rooted in the constant barrage of **propaganda** directed at the Baltic States. Because of their close cultural ties to the West, Communist Party leaders feared that the Lithuanian people would be seduced by the comparative wealth of nearby **capitalist** countries such as Finland. State-owned Lithuanian television broadcast images of inner-city poverty,

IN HOC SIGNO VINCES

Sometimes called the "Mecca of Lithuania," the Hill of Crosses is estimated to contain at least half a million crosses. The site, located about 6.2 miles (10 kilometers) north of Siauliai, is a testament to the faith of the Lithuanian people.

bag ladies, and race riots in the United States to help promote an image of the West as corrupt and dangerous.

By the 1980s however, these images and ideas were losing their power. Baltic **dissidents** began to hold public protests in Riga, Tallinn, and Vilnius. In 1988, against the wishes of the communist regime, Lithuanians engaged in a peaceful protest through a nationwide celebration of the February 16, 1918, declaration of independence. Lithuanian intellectuals soon began to take more forceful action. Meeting at the National Academy of Sciences on June 3, 1988, communist and noncommunist intellectuals formed "an initiative group" to organize a society to support Soviet leader Mikhail Gorbachev's program of **glasnost**, democratization, and **perestroika**. A council composed equally of Communist Party members and nonparty members was chosen to form the Lithuanian Reconstruction Movement, which eventually became known simply as Sajudis.

Sajudis supported Gorbachev's policies, but at the same time it promoted domestic Lithuanian national issues such as restoration of the Lithuanian language as the "official" language. When elections were eventually held for representatives to the newly formed Congress of People's Deputies in 1989, Sajudis members overwhelmingly beat communist candidates. Lithuanian sovereignty (which Lithuanians viewed as separate from independence, already declared on February 16, 1918) was proclaimed in May 1989, and Lithuania's incorporation into the Soviet Union was declared illegal. That August, a human chain linked the three Baltic capitals of Tallinn, Riga, and Vilnius to commemorate the fiftieth anniversary of the infamous Molotov-Ribbentrop Pact. Finally, on March 11, 1990, a newly elected parliament voted unanimously to reinstate independence.

Unfortunately, the Soviets did not accept the independence vote. In April 1990, they imposed an economic blockade that lasted for three months, forcing the Lithuanian legislature, now known as the Supreme Council, to agree to a six-month freeze on its independence declaration. Later, Moscow attempted to use force to remove the Lithuanian government in Vilnius and to reestablish Soviet rule. This attempted coup ended in a massacre where thirteen civilians died, and hundreds more were wounded by the Soviet Army. This tragedy only served to strengthen the resolve of the Lithuanian people.

Ultimately, the collapse of the communist government in Moscow permitted Lithuania to regain self-determination and prompted the international community to recognize it as an independent state. Lithuania was admitted to the United Nations on September 16, 1991, and today is a member of NATO and the EU. After a long history of foreign domination and conflict, Lithuania has made great strides in its political and economic development. It is now a free and independent country, looking forward to the future as an active member of the global community of nations.

The center of Vilnius is preserved by strict architectural guidelines, while new construction booms in other parts of the city.

3 CHAPTER THE ECONOMY

Lithuania is emerging from a period of economic difficulty that marked its independence from Soviet control. Many challenges continue to face the Lithuanian economy, although great strides have been made to implement a **market economy** that is competitive with the economies of greater Europe.

Transition to a Market Economy

For much of the last century, Lithuania's economy operated on the communist model. Under Soviet communism, all enterprise was owned by the state, and all economic policy was established in Moscow. This central planning was very ineffective, since it did not take into account local needs or strengths. Also, by removing any sense of control from the local population, the Lithuanian people took little interest in developing new or more efficient means of production. As a result, when communism came to an end, Lithuania was left with an **infrastructure** that was inadequate to compete in the world marketplace. Rapid reforms were needed to adapt to the rigors of a market economy.

The two main components of a market economy are **entrepreneurial** responsibility and competition. It is an entrepreneur's responsibility to monitor the company's growth and to ensure that it can adapt to changing circumstances. Competition ensures that new products and technologies will constantly be developed as each business works to ensure that its product best meets the needs of the end consumer. The government's role is limited to creating conditions favorable to a healthy economy by contributing to the infrastructure, as well as fair labor and tax laws. The government also provides assistance to those unable to cope with the greater demands of a competitive market.

Making the change from a centrally planned economy to a market economy presents great challenges. Immediately following the collapse of the Soviet system, the Lithuanian economy experienced a number of major setbacks. Lithuania suffered a major decrease in its exports to the former Soviet Union, and many industries were unable to sell a large portion of their production. Energy prices skyrocketed, and unemployment reached an all-time high. Today, however, the situation has improved tremendously. In the mid-1990s, growth in the newly emerging **service sector** helped fuel a recovery. Unemployment has dropped, and foreign aid has helped to rebuild the nation's deteriorating infrastructure. This in turn has paved the way for increased foreign investment. The Lithuanian economy has improved steadily and has established a pattern of consistent growth over the last five years.

The New Economy

Although nearly one-third of Lithuania's **gross domestic product (GDP)** comes from its manufacturing industries, the primary source of

Lithuanians know that the task of rebuilding their nation after years of subjugation will require both muscle-power and good planning.

Lithuania's income today comes from the service sector, which contributes more than 60 percent of the country's GDP. This includes the country's wholesale and retail trade, transport, shipping, and storage, as well as the emerging sectors of communications, ***information technology***, and tourism.

Lithuania's banking system has also undergone systematic reform since the fall of communism. EU membership requires an efficient and

Heavy industry is one of the mainstays of the Lithuanian economy.
More than 30 percent of the nation's gross domestic product depends on this sector.

open financial market and a stable banking system. Lithuania's reform program included changes in the country's bank-licensing system. **Privatization** of the three major state banks has also been completed. The government has agreed to pass stronger bankruptcy legislation and to guarantee its enforcement. Today, the Bank of Lithuania is the major financial services provider in the country, and interest rates have stabilized enough to make credit cards and other forms of banking services more readily available.

INDUSTRY: A CRITICAL SECTOR OF THE ECONOMY

Heavy industry is still an important part of Latvia's economy. Thirty-one percent of the country's GDP is dependent on the export of heavy machinery, electronics, refrigerators and freezers, petroleum products, textiles, food processing, fertilizers, agricultural machinery, optical equipment, computers, and amber. Shipbuilding and furniture making are also important industries, with shipbuilding in particular seeing increased growth due to foreign investment.

During the Soviet era, Lithuanian industries were developed to meet the needs of consumers within the Soviet Union itself. Following independence, many of these products could not compete with superior products being produced more efficiently in the West. Today, many of these factories are being updated to produce different products that are more competitive in world markets.

QUICK FACTS: THE ECONOMY OF LITHUANIA

Gross Domestic Product (GDP): US$45.23 billion
GDP per capita: US$12,500
Industries: metal-cutting machine tools, electric motors, television sets, refrigerators and freezers, petroleum refining, shipbuilding, furniture making, textiles, food processing, fertilizers, agricultural machinery, optical equipment, electronic components, computers, amber
Agriculture: grain, potatoes, sugar beets, flax, vegetables, beef, milk, eggs, fish
Export commodities: mineral products, textiles and clothing, machinery and equipment, chemicals, wood and wood products, foodstuffs (2001)
Export partners: Switzerland 11.6%, Russia 10.1%, Germany 9.9%, Latvia 9.7%, UK 6.4%, France 5.1%, Denmark 4.7%, Estonia 4.3%, Sweden 4% (2003)
Import commodities: mineral products, machinery and equipment, transport equipment, chemicals, textiles and clothing, metals (2001)
Import partners: Russia 22%, Germany 16.1%, Poland 5.2%, Italy 4.3%, France 4.2% (2003)
Currency: Litas (LTL)
Currency exchange rate: US$1 = 2.83 LTL (June 9, 2005)

Note: All figures are from 2004 unless otherwise indicated.
Source: www.cia.gov, 2005.

AGRICULTURE

Agriculture accounts for more than 8 percent of the GDP. Lithuanian farmers produce wheat, rye, barley, feed grains, potatoes, flax, and sugar beets. Other agricultural enterprises include dairy farming, meat production, and food processing. Although Lithuania has succeeded in privatizing more agricultural land than its neighbors in Estonia or Latvia, agricultural production has decreased by more than 50 percent since 1989. One problem is that large, government-owned collective farms were broken up into small private holdings, often not large enough to be economically viable. A serious drought in 1994 further reduced agricultural production and cost farmers the equivalent of US$280 million in lost crops.

A mounting concern after EU accession is the small size of most modern Lithuanian farms, many of which will not be large enough to receive EU **subsidies** without a significant investment. It is feared that the majority of small farmers, too poor to expand to the size necessary to meet EU quotas, will suffer as cheaper food stuffs are imported from other EU nations.

ENERGY SOURCES

Lithuania receives more than 87 percent of its electricity from the Ignalina nuclear power plant. Unfortunately, Lithuania is highly dependent on fuels imported from foreign countries, especially Russia, and this energy dependence plagues Lithuania's industries. A large portion of the electricity produced at the 5,680-megawatt Ignalina nuclear power plant is exported to Belarus, Latvia, and Kaliningrad Oblast in Russia, although exports have decreased in recent years. Lithuania has large processing facilities for oil, which can be exported to the West through Latvia or the new Lithuanian transport and storage facility at Butinge. The new facility was constructed by Western firms with funding provided by international financial institutions.

The availability of transport and storage facilities within Lithuania itself may allow the oil-processing plant at Mazeikiai to operate profitably. Mazeikiai needs upgrading but has an annual capacity of twelve million tons, making it one of the largest oil-processing plants in the Baltic region. Lithuania has moderate oil and gas deposits offshore and on the Baltic coast. The nation's recoverable oil reserves are estimated at forty million tons on the coast and thirty-eight million tons offshore.

Environmental protection and reducing dependence on foreign imports are among the most important factors of Lithuania's new, EU-driven energy policy, and it hopes to secure EU funds for

The seaport of Klaipeda is the only seaport of Lithuania, its gateway to the Baltic. Through this port, much of Lithuania's industrial production is shipped on freighters.

environmental cleanup as well as research into supplies of renewable energy. The Soviet era has left a legacy of environmental damage in Lithuania. Although reforms have been made to bring conditions in Lithuania in line with those in other EU member nations, a great deal of work remains to be done.

TRANSPORTATION AND COMMUNICATIONS

Lithuania's transportation system has great potential, and shipping by rail, road, and ship represents an important part of Lithuania's future economic development. Highways, railways,

The houses in the village of Nida, located on the Curonian Spit, retain their quaint 19th century style, although they possess modern appliances and plumbing.

waterways (both navigable rivers and seaports), and airports make up Lithuania's transportation system. Transportation is critical to a competitive economy, and as a result, great investments are being made in updating the nation's transportation system. The main international airport is in Vilnius, and a second international airport was opened at Siauliai in 1993. In addition to Lithuanian Airlines, service is provided by Aeroflot, Austrian Airlines, Drakk Air Lines, Hamburg Airlines, LOT (Polish Airlines), Lufthansa, Malév, SAS (Scandinavian Airlines), and Swissair. The Via Baltica is a major international roadway, linking all three Baltic States with Scandinavia and Central Europe.

The communications infrastructure is also undergoing a period of dramatic change. Lithuania's telephone service is among the most advanced in the former Soviet republics. In the early 1990s, 240 telephone lines served one thousand homes. Recent legislation has allowed both basic telephone service and long distance service to expand throughout most of the country. Lithuania has two television networks and five radio stations. Services such as Internet access and wireless telephone service are also being expanded but are currently available only in the most urban areas.

LOOKING AHEAD

As Lithuania enters a new period of economic growth and begins to take advantage of the opportunities provided by its membership in the EU, the outlook for prosperity and an increased standard of living is bright. Challenges still remain, and much work remains before Lithuania is truly an equal partner with the more prosperous nations of the West.

Lithuanian culture retains its links to the land, with many people pursuing traditional pastimes in the countryside.

4 LITHUANIA'S PEOPLE AND CULTURE

The Lithuanian people are generally ethnically and culturally **homogeneous** and overwhelmingly Roman Catholic. This has given them a strong sense of unity that has allowed Lithuanian language, culture, and traditions to survive centuries of foreign influences. The Lithuanians also have a strong national identity and are proud of their rich heritage.

Lithuania was the last nation in Europe to adopt the Christian faith. Nowadays, many Lithuanians are members of the Catholic Church.

RELIGION: FREEDOM OF CHOICE

Today, the Lithuanian people have full freedom to choose their faith and religion. Traditionally, Lithuania has been a Roman Catholic country. Despite the harsh repression of the Soviet years, the Roman Catholic Church remains the nation's most dominant and influential faith. In the past, Lithuania has had two small but active Protestant denominations, the Evangelical Reformed Church and the Evangelical Lutheran. In addition, Orthodox Christianity and Judaism have roots at

least as old as those of Roman Catholicism. Baptists, Karaites, Pentecostals, Seventh-day Adventists, and even Islam and Hare Krishna have a presence in Lithuania today.

FOOD AND DRINK: SIMPLE FARE

The traditional Lithuanian diet has always varied according to season. Animals were slaughtered in the fall and winter, so more meat was eaten at those times. Milk, vegetables, berries, mushrooms, and various flour-based dishes were more abundant in the spring and summer. Black rye bread is an ancient staple food and can still be found on Lithuanian tables. Historically, Lithuanians baked white bread only for special occasions.

Porridges are made from a number of different grains. Flour pancakes are common throughout the country. Dairy products are also an important part of Lithuanian cuisine, which relies heavily on milk, butter, sour cream, and homemade cheeses. A common favorite is cold beet soup with cucumbers, dill, and eggs served alongside a dish of hot boiled potatoes. Fresh and pickled cabbage soups are also popular. Milk-based soups with potatoes, peas, carrots, cabbages, or pieces of flour dough are often served for dinner. Meat is of lesser importance in Lithuanian cuisine, owing in part to its lack of availability in the days before modern conveniences like refrigeration. Pork and bacon are enjoyed boiled or baked. For longer storage, these meats are salted down for several weeks in large troughs or vats and then smoked. *Skilandis*, a favorite Lithuanian delicacy, consists of coarsely chopped pork, garlic, pepper, and salt tightly packed into a pig stomach and smoked.

Special meals are prepared to commemorate holidays and important events. Strict etiquette is observed for these holiday feasts, and families travel great distances to celebrate together. Even death is not considered important enough to excuse one from attendance at a family gathering, and places are set for the dead and left empty at the traditional Lithuanian table.

EDUCATION: A RETURN TO TRADITIONAL STUDIES

Lithuanians take education very seriously. Almost all adults can read and write, and most can speak at least two languages. In Lithuania, education is **compulsory** and every child between ages six and sixteen must attend school. The school system, though, is quite different from most in North America. All Lithuanian children attend *Pradiné Mokykla*, or primary school, from ages six to eleven. After Pradiné Mokykla, the students are divided into two different school streams. Some stu-

cational program, implemented by the Soviets, to a more Western model, taught in the Lithuanian language.

AUGURY: A LEGACY OF THE PAGAN PAST

Traditional Lithuanian peasant culture has been preserved in many forms. Although the celebrations and rituals that once were the cornerstones of this agrarian society have lost their place in everyday life, remnants of the past can still be found, particularly in the celebrations of Lithuanian holidays and feasts. An important aspect of this is **augury**, where customs were designed to help foretell the future. Many Lithuanian cultural traditions have their roots in Lithuania's past as the last nation to convert from paganism to Christianity. Pagan rituals and customs were merged with the rites of the Roman Catholic Church to create the traditions that are observed today.

dents go to *Pagrindiné Mokykla*, which provides a basic education program. The remaining students enroll in the *Viduriné Mokykla, Gimnazija,* an academic, college-preparatory school. The Lithuanian school system is still undergoing changes as it converts from a Russian-based edu-

Christmas Eve traditions in Lithuania provide a glimpse into such practices. For example, it is thought that on Christmas Eve, spirits return to their homes. Because of this, one should not travel far from home for fear of meeting hostile spirits.

Lithuania is undergoing a fundamental transition, like all of Eastern Europe, and new graffiti coexists with Soviet-era statuary.

The brothers Valentinas and Jonas Simonelis both exhibit their sculpture in the Lithuanian capital of Vilnius. For years, they maintained an informal museum that housed bells that had been confiscated from churches. Now, however, the bells have been returned to their rightful homes, and the museum is used to show modern sculpture.

A special Christmas Eve feast is held each year, and many families still celebrate in a traditional fashion. Special wafers with nativity scenes are shared among members of the family, and the size of the piece you receive is thought to be an indicator of your luck for the following year.

The traditional Christmas dining table was covered with hay and usually set with twelve meatless dishes, one for each of the twelve apostles. The hay was meant to symbolize the manger. After dinner, people pulled hay stalks from under the tablecloth to forecast their fortunes. A long stem meant good fortune and a long life, whereas a short one meant that that person might not live to see the next Christmas. Unmarried girls then went out to gather logs for the fire. It was important to gather as many as one could carry. Once inside the logs were counted; even numbers meant that the girl would marry soon, whereas odd numbers signified that they'd remain single in the following year.

Most other Lithuanian celebrations are also marked by rituals to predict future events, such as births, marriages, deaths, and the success or failure of crops. Once strictly observed, these customs now represent a fun and playful way for Lithuanians to connect with the beliefs and mysticism of the past.

MUSIC: CULTURAL IDENTITY THROUGH SONG

Traditional Lithuanian folk music has played a critical role in preserving the language, culture, and history of the Lithuanian people. More than just widely recognized songs sung to a familiar melody, Lithuanian folk music distinguishes itself through ancient **polyphonic** melodies that may seem **dissonant** to modern listeners. Thousands of these songs have been passed down as an oral tradition for more than one thousand years. Popular themes are farming, marriage and love, pregnancy, childbirth, aging, and death.

Very specific songs are sung to mark religious occasions such as baptisms, weddings, and funerals. Some of the newer songs are sung in two parts, with the second voice issuing a response to the first. The lyrics are typically full of metaphor and symbolism. Another unique feature of Lithuanian music is its focus on daily life from a woman's perspective. War songs, for example, do not glorify bravery and death but rather emphasize the loss suffered by those left behind. Work, thrift, and industriousness are often praised. The ancient nature of Lithuanian culture is highlighted by this music, which is the oral history of the Lithuanian people, predating written history. Even today, Lithuanian women often can recite from memory more than one hundred different songs; accomplished singers of the past could recite more than four hundred. This important part of Lithuanian culture has helped the language and traditions of Lithuania to survive the ravages of history.

The cities in Lithuania were magnets for population growth during Soviet times,
but since independence there has been a migration to the countryside.

5 THE CITIES

During Soviet rule, industrialization brought about fast and sustained urban development in Lithuania. Until Lithuania regained its independence, nearly 1 percent of the rural population had moved to cities every year since 1950. However, after achieving independence, a shift has been seen as more people migrate back to rural areas to take advantage of the privatization

St. Casmir's, the oldest Baroque church in Vilnius, served for two decades as a museum of atheism when the Soviets ruled Lithuania. Now, it is being reconstructed, but still is closed to visitors.

of formerly state-owned farms. Still, nearly 70 percent of Lithuanians live around urban centers. These are not large metropolises like New York, London, Paris, or Rome, but rather small cities where jobs are more readily available. Even the cities in Lithuania retain a certain amount of rural character.

VILNIUS: THE CAPITAL

Vilnius, Lithuania's capital and most populated city, is situated in southeastern Lithuania where the River Vilnia meets the River Neris. The earliest archaeological findings in the city prove that the area has been inhabited since the early Middle Ages. Initially a Baltic settlement, it was also inhabited by Slavs. Some historians identify the city with Voruta, the forgotten capital of King Mindaugas. Written references to the city first appear in 1323.

As a city that has survived for more than six hundred years, it is not surprising that Vilnius boasts a host of important historical sites. The old town, historical center of Vilnius, is one of the largest in Europe. The most valuable historic and cultural sites are concentrated here. The nearly 1,500 buildings in the old town were built over the span of centuries, creating a splendid blend of many different architectural styles. Although Vilnius is often called a Baroque city, it also has some Gothic and Renaissance buildings. The main sights of the city are the Gediminas Castle and the Cathedral Square.

Vilnius is also the home of Lithuania's cultural life. With twenty-two museums, thirteen art galleries, a host of professional theaters, cinemas, and concert halls, an important cultural or educational event is always taking place. Vilnius is also home to Vilnius University, the country's oldest and largest university center. Since independence, Lithuania has worked to bring attention to Vilnius as a tourist destination, and tourism has increased dramatically as thousands of tourists from around the world come to experience the many wonders of this ancient city.

KAUNAS: A CENTER FOR EDUCATION

Kaunas, the second-largest city in Lithuania (400,000 inhabitants) is an ancient city famous for its many historic buildings and monuments. Some of the most prominent include the remains of Kaunas Castle, built in the thirteenth century, which stands near the point where Lithuania's two largest rivers (the Nemunas and Neris) meet; the Old Town Hall, which stands in the center of Rotuses Square; and the impressive seventeenth-century

The *Meridianas Ship*, as this boat is now known, was built in 1948, and originally owned by Finns, who used it in a navigation school. For years afterward, the ship was a floating restaurant, and fell into disrepair. A local businessman recently bought the ship, and has outfitted it with sails provided by a Lithuanian beer company.

Jesuit church. The entire historic district is connected by a winding maze of cobblestone streets lined with facades dating back to the seventeenth century.

Among Lithuanians, Kaunas is known as the nation's center for higher education. More than thirty-five thousand students live in Kaunas and study at one of the city's nine colleges and universities. The city is also an important industrial center, with large textile factories and several food processing plants.

KLAIPEDA: AN IMPORTANT SEAPORT

Klaipeda is Lithuania's only seaport. Located on the Baltic Sea, Klaipeda is a major ferry port with connections to Sweden, Denmark, and Germany. It is situated close to the mouth of the Curonian Lagoon. Klaipeda, with its population of 205,000, ranks third among the cities of Lithuania and is one of the most important cities of the republic. It is an important sea transport center with an international ferry port, oil export, commercial and fishing ports, and shipbuilding and ship-repairing, fish and food processing, and wood and furniture industries.

The city also has a rich cultural life and boasts a major university, several other colleges and vocational schools, concert halls, drama theatres, museums, libraries, the Art Exhibition Palace, a number of smaller art galleries, as well as the park of sculptures, the carillon, and many other historical and cultural monuments. The area is noted for its beaches and other natural treasures. The city is also home to the national Maritime Museum and Aquarium.

SIAULIAI AND PANEVEZYS: IMPORTANT INDUSTRIAL CENTERS

Lithuania's fourth-largest city, Siauliai, is situated at the junction of two roads that in ancient times, were used by hunters, warriors, and merchants. Today these roads connect Tallin and Warsaw, and run west to the seaport of Klaipeda and east to Russia through Latvia. Due to its perfect geographical location, Siauliai became the primary trade and industrial center in Lithuania from the very start.

Today, Siauliai remains a hub of economic activity, producing items as varied as TV sets, bicycles, leather goods and footwear, knitwear, machine tools, metal items, furniture, and food. The economic, cultural, and educational center of northern Lithuania, the city is home to twenty-three secondary schools, six colleges, and a private business school.

Panevezys, Lithuania's fifth-largest city, is located halfway between two Baltic capitals, Vilnius and Riga. The Via Baltica International Highway runs through the city, and railroads lead to Klaipeda in the West and to the many cities in the East. This transportation network has been critical to the rapid development of industry in the region. A major industrial city, electronics, glass, textile, furniture, construction, food, and other industries can all be found in Panevezys.

The EU flag

6 THE FORMATION OF THE EUROPEAN UNION

The EU is an economic and political confederation of twenty-five European nations. Member countries abide by common foreign and security policies and cooperate on judicial and domestic affairs. The confederation, however, does not replace existing states or governments. Each of the twenty-five member states is *autonomous*, but they have all agreed to establish some common institutions and to hand over some of their own decision-making powers to these international bodies. As a result, decisions on matters that interest all member states can be made democratically, accommodating everyone's concerns and interests.

Today, the EU is the most powerful regional organization in the world. It has evolved from a primarily economic organization to an increasingly political one. Besides promoting economic cooperation, the EU requires that its members uphold fundamental values of peace and **solidarity**, human dignity, freedom, and equality. Based on the principles of democracy and the rule of law, the EU respects the culture and organizations of member states.

HISTORY

The seeds of the EU were planted more than fifty years ago in a Europe reduced to smoking piles of rubble by two world wars. European nations suffered great financial difficulties in the postwar period. They were struggling to get back on their feet and realized that another war would cause further hardship. Knowing that internal conflict was hurting all of Europe, a drive began toward European cooperation.

France took the first historic step. On May 9, 1950 (now celebrated as Europe Day), Robert Schuman, the French foreign minister, proposed the coal and steel industries of France and West Germany be coordinated under a single supranational authority. The proposal, known as the Treaty of Paris, attracted four other countries—Belgium, Luxembourg, the Netherlands, and Italy—and resulted in the 1951 formation of the European Coal and Steel Community (ECSC). These six countries became the founding members of the EU.

In 1957, European cooperation took its next big leap. Under the Treaty of Rome, the European Economic Community (EEC) and the European Atomic Energy Community (EURATOM) were formed. Informally known as the Common Market, the EEC promoted joining the national economies into a single European economy. The 1965 Treaty of Brussels (more commonly referred to as the Merger Treaty) united these various treaty organizations under a single umbrella, the European Community (EC).

In 1992, the Maastricht Treaty (also known as the Treaty of the European Union) was signed in Maastricht, the Netherlands, signaling the birth of the EU as it stands today. **Ratified** the following year, the Maastricht Treaty provided for a central banking system, a common currency (the euro) to replace the national currencies, a legal definition of the EU, and a framework for expanding the

The EU's united economy has allowed it to become a worldwide financial power.

EU's political role, particularly in the area of foreign and security policy.

By 1993, the member countries completed their move toward a single market and agreed to participate in a larger common market, the European Economic Area, established in 1994.

The EU, headquartered in Brussels, Belgium, reached its current member strength in spurts. In

© BCE ECB EZB EKT EKP 2002

© BCE ECB EZB EKT EKP 2002

© BCE ECB EZB EKT EKP 2002

© BCE ECB EZB EKT EKP 2002

The euro, the EU's currency

1973, Denmark, Ireland, and the United Kingdom joined the six founding members of the EC. They were followed by Greece in 1981, and Portugal and Spain in 1986. The 1990s saw the unification of the two Germanys, and as a result, East Germany entered the EU fold. Austria, Finland, and Sweden joined the EU in 1995, bringing the total number of member states to fifteen. In 2004, the EU nearly doubled its size when ten countries—Cyprus, the Czech Republic, Estonia, Hungary, Latvia, Lithuania, Malta, Poland, Slovakia, and Slovenia—became members.

THE EU FRAMEWORK

The EU's structure has often been compared to a "roof of a temple with three columns." As established by the Maastricht Treaty, this three-pillar framework encompasses all the policy areas—or pillars—of European cooperation. The three pillars of the EU are the European Community, the Common Foreign and Security Policy (CFSP), and Police and Judicial Co-operation in Criminal Matters.

QUICK FACTS: THE EUROPEAN UNION

Number of Member Countries: 25
Official Languages: 20—Czech, Danish, Dutch, English, Estonian, Finnish, French, German, Greek, Hungarian, Italian, Latvian, Lithuanian, Maltese, Polish, Portuguese, Slovak, Slovenian, Spanish, and Swedish; additional language for treaty purposes: Irish Gaelic
Motto: *In Varietate Concordia* (United in Diversity)
European Council's President: Each member state takes a turn to lead the council's activities for 6 months.
European Commission's President: José Manuel Barroso (Portugal)
European Parliament's President: Josep Borrell (Spain)
Total Area: 1,502,966 square miles (3,892,685 sq. km.)
Population: 454,900,000
Population Density: 302.7 people/square mile (116.8 people/sq. km.)
GDP: €9.61.1012
Per Capita GDP: €21,125
Formation:
- Declared: February 7, 1992, with signing of the Maastricht Treaty
- Recognized: November 1, 1993, with the ratification of the Maastricht Treaty

Community Currency: Euro. Currently 12 of the 25 member states have adopted the euro as their currency.
Anthem: "Ode to Joy"
Flag: Blue background with 12 gold stars arranged in a circle
Official Day: Europe Day, May 9

Source: europa.eu.int

PILLAR ONE

The European Community pillar deals with economic, social, and environmental policies. It is a body consisting of the European Parliament, European Commission, European Court of Justice, Council of the European Union, and the European Courts of Auditors.

PILLAR TWO

The idea that the EU should speak with one voice in world affairs is as old as the European integration process itself. Toward this end, the Common Foreign and Security Policy (CFSP) was formed in 1993.

PILLAR THREE

The cooperation of EU member states in judicial and criminal matters ensures that its citizens enjoy the freedom to travel, work, and live securely and safely anywhere within the EU. The third pillar—Police and Judicial Co-operation in Criminal Matters—helps to protect EU citizens from international crime and to ensure equal access to justice and fundamental rights across the EU.

The flags of the EU's nations:

top row, left to right
Belgium, the Czech Republic, Denmark, Germany, Estonia, Greece

second row, left to right
Spain, France, Ireland, Italy, Cyprus, Latvia

third row, left to right
Lithuania, Luxembourg, Hungary, Malta, the Netherlands, Austria

bottom row, left to right
Poland, Portugal, Slovenia, Slovakia, Finland, Sweden, United Kingdom

ECONOMIC STATUS

As of May 2004, the EU had the largest economy in the world, followed closely by the United States. But even though the EU continues to enjoy a trade surplus, it faces the twin problems of high unemployment rates and **stagnancy**.

The 2004 addition of ten new member states is expected to boost economic growth. EU membership is likely to stimulate the economies of these relatively poor countries. In turn, their prosperity growth will be beneficial to the EU.

THE EURO

The EU's official currency is the euro, which came into circulation on January 1, 2002. The shift to the euro has been the largest monetary changeover in the world. Twelve countries—Belgium, Germany, Greece, Spain, France, Ireland, Italy, Luxembourg, the Netherlands, Finland, Portugal, and Austria—have adopted it as their currency.

SINGLE MARKET

Within the EU, laws of member states are harmonized and domestic policies are coordinated to create a larger, more-efficient single market.

The chief features of the EU's internal policy on the single market are:

- free trade of goods and services

- a common EU competition law that controls anticompetitive activities of companies and member states

- removal of internal border control and harmonization of external controls between member states

- freedom for citizens to live and work anywhere in the EU as long as they are not dependent on the state

- free movement of **capital** between member states

- harmonization of government regulations, corporation law, and trademark registration

- a single currency

- coordination of environmental policy

- a common agricultural policy and a common fisheries policy

- a common system of indirect taxation, the value-added tax (VAT), and common customs duties and **excise**

- funding for research

- funding for aid to disadvantaged regions

The EU's external policy on the single market specifies:

- a common external **tariff** and a common position in international trade negotiations

- funding of programs in other Eastern European countries and developing countries

COOPERATION AREAS

EU member states cooperate in other areas as well. Member states can vote in European Parliament elections. Intelligence sharing and cooperation in criminal matters are carried out through EUROPOL and the Schengen Information System.

The EU is working to develop common foreign and security policies. Many member states are resisting such a move, however, saying these are sensitive areas best left to individual member states. Arguing in favor of a common approach to security and foreign policy are countries like France and Germany, who insist that a safer and more secure Europe can only become a reality under the EU umbrella.

One of the EU's great achievements has been to create a boundary-free area within which people, goods, services, and money can move around freely; this ease of movement is sometimes called "the four freedoms." As the EU grows in size, so do the challenges facing it—and yet its fifty-year history has amply demonstrated the power of cooperation.

Europe is proud of its "bright idea," a union with economic and political power.

The EU believes that it can use its power to act as a "lighthouse" for the rest of the world.

KEY EU INSTITUTIONS

Five key institutions play a specific role in the EU.

THE EUROPEAN PARLIAMENT

The European Parliament (EP) is the democratic voice of the people of Europe. Directly elected every five years, the Members of the European Parliament (MEPs) sit not in national **blocs** but in political groups representing the seven main political parties of the member states. Each group reflects the political ideology of the national parties to which its members belong. Some MEPs are not attached to any political group.

COUNCIL OF THE EUROPEAN UNION

The Council of the European Union (formerly known as the Council of Ministers) is the main leg-

islative and decision-making body in the EU. It brings together the nationally elected representatives of the member-state governments. One minister from each of the EU's member states attends council meetings. It is the forum in which government representatives can assert their interests and reach compromises. Increasingly, the Council of the European Union and the EP are acting together as colegislators in decision-making processes.

EUROPEAN COMMISSION

The European Commission does much of the day-to-day work of the EU. Politically independent, the commission represents the interests of the EU as a whole, rather than those of individual member states. It drafts proposals for new European laws, which it presents to the EP and the Council of the European Union. The European Commission makes sure EU decisions are implemented properly and supervises the way EU funds are spent. It also sees that everyone abides by the European treaties and European law.

The EU member-state governments choose the European Commission president, who is then approved by the EP. Member states, in consultation with the incoming president, nominate the other European Commission members, who must also be approved by the EP. The commission is appointed for a five-year term, but can be dismissed by the EP. Many members of its staff work in Brussels, Belgium.

COURT OF JUSTICE

Headquartered in Luxembourg, the Court of Justice of the European Communities consists of one independent judge from each EU country. This court ensures that the common rules decided in the EU are understood and followed uniformly by all the members. The Court of Justice settles disputes over how EU treaties and legislation are interpreted. If national courts are in doubt about how to apply EU rules, they must ask the Court of Justice. Individuals can also bring proceedings against EU institutions before the court.

COURT OF AUDITORS

EU funds must be used legally, economically, and for their intended purpose. The Court of Auditors, an independent EU institution located in Luxembourg, is responsible for overseeing how EU money is spent. In effect, these auditors help European taxpayers get better value for the money that has been channeled into the EU.

OTHER IMPORTANT BODIES

1. European Economic and Social Committee: expresses the opinions of organized civil society on economic and social issues

2. Committee of the Regions: expresses the opinions of regional and local authorities

3. European Central Bank: responsible for monetary policy and managing the euro

4. European Ombudsman: deals with citizens' complaints about mismanagement by any EU institution or body

5. European Investment Bank: helps achieve EU objectives by financing investment projects

Together with a number of agencies and other bodies completing the system, the EU's institutions have made it the most powerful organization in the world.

EU Member States

In order to become a member of the EU, a country must have a stable democracy that guarantees the rule of law, human rights, and protection of minorities. It must also have a functioning market economy as well as a civil service capable of applying and managing EU laws.

The EU provides substantial financial assistance and advice to help candidate countries prepare themselves for membership. As of October 2004, the EU has twenty-five member states. Bulgaria and Romania are likely to join in 2007, which would bring the EU's total population to nearly 500 million.

In December 2004, the EU decided to open negotiations with Turkey on its proposed membership. Turkey's possible entry into the EU has been fraught with controversy. Much of this controversy has centered on Turkey's human rights record and the divided island of Cyprus. If allowed to join the EU, Turkey would be its most-populous member state.

The 2004 expansion was the EU's most ambitious enlargement to date. Never before has the EU embraced so many new countries, grown so much in terms of area and population, or encompassed so many different histories and cultures. As the EU moves forward into the twenty-first century, it will undoubtedly continue to grow in both political and economic strength.

The sculpture garden maintained by Jonas and Valentinas Simonelis in the village of Sirutenai shows the importance that Lithuanians attach to the fine arts.

7 LITHUANIA IN THE EUROPEAN UNION

Ten new member nations were admitted to the EU in 2004. These nations were Lithuania, Cyprus, Estonia, Hungary, Slovakia, Latvia, Malta, Poland, the Czech Republic, and Slovenia. As a relatively new member of the EU, Lithuania is undergoing a critical period of growth as it adjusts to the new economic and political situation.

LITHUANIA AND EU ACCESSION

In the wake of the collapse of the Soviet Union, Latvia faced many economic and political challenges. Having identified themselves more with the nations of Western Europe than with Russia in the east, Lithuanians were eager to restore what they saw as traditional ties with their neighbors in the West. Membership in NATO and the EU became Lithuania's top foreign policy priorities.

In 2003, following a transition period of sweeping economic and political reforms, Lithuanians voted for membership in the EU in a historic **referendum**. Although national polls showed that some citizens had concerns about joining the EU, most felt that tapping into the resources of a wider Europe would bring their new country more advantages than disadvantages. The process of joining the EU, called accession, requires that potential members adopt common policies on a wide variety of issues, from trade and commerce to environmental protection and human rights.

DIFFERING VIEWS OF A UNITED EUROPE

Public opinion in Europe remains divided about the amount of decision-making control member nations should surrender to the EU. Most Lithuanians want to surrender a minimum of sovereignty, especially over such things as defense and foreign policy. Concern has been expressed that as a nation that has only recently gained a democratically elected legislative body, the Lithuanian voting public should have more control over legislation being passed than the European Parliament in Brussels. Currently Lithuania and many of the other new EU states support a policy termed intergovernmentalism—a governmental approach in which member states must decide on policy by unanimous agreement. Lithuanians remain concerned that their status as a new member of the EU and their relative economic weakness put their interests behind the interests of larger countries like Germany in EU decision making.

Others, primarily in the larger EU countries, feel strongly that the greatest opportunities for growth can be found within the framework of a strongly united Europe. Supporters of supranationalism—a governmental approach in which EU member states would be bound by decisions based on majority rule—believe that the benefits of having common policies for defense, treaty negotiation, and trade far outweigh the individual interests of separate member states.

BENEFITS OF EU MEMBERSHIP

EU membership is expected to have a tremendous impact on the standard of living in many parts of Lithuania.

Lithuanians have mixed opinions about what to expect from European Union membership. There are hopes and fears about the future.

For example, great discrepancies exist between the standard of living enjoyed by urban Lithuanians, such as those living in Vilnius, and the conditions faced by poorer citizens in the more rural areas of the country. Many of the roadways are still suffering from decades-old neglect that originated during the Soviet era. This complicates the commercial transport of goods and services.

Access to communications is limited in some parts of the country.

As a new member of the EU, Lithuania will be able to access millions of dollars in additional funding provided to develop an infrastructure that is comparable to the rest of Europe. The funds are allocated to help address the economic and social inequalities between the richest and poorest EU nations. This money will be used to support agriculture, build new roads and bridges, improve health-care and social welfare programs, and improve environmental conditions. All these improvements are designed to promote continued foreign investment.

With the financial assistance Lithuanians receive from the EU helping to create a favorable business environment, the country will be able to lower its own corporate taxes in hope of luring companies away from areas where it is more expensive to do business. The potential of economic assistance to help equal the playing field between Lithuania and its neighbors to the west was one of the strongest motivating factors behind the decision to move forward with EU accession.

Lithuania can also apply to the EU for millions in research dollars. The EU is a large source of

After years of repression of religion, many Lithuanians are now grateful to worship according to the faith of their choosing.

funding for all types of scientific investigation. Large sums of money are available to promote the development of **sustainable** agriculture, alternative energy sources, and medicine.

AREAS OF CONCERN

Although Lithuania has much to gain by its membership in the EU, lingering concerns persist that not all areas of society will benefit from membership. One element of EU membership that was once perceived to be a great benefit to Lithuanian workers was the free movement of labor. In theory, workers from one EU country could freely move to another EU member nation to find work without having to go through normal immigration procedures. For many unemployed or low-earning workers, the possibility of relocating freely to neighboring states with higher wages and better standards of living was very appealing, especially for those Lithuanian citizens of minority backgrounds who sought to leave the country anyway.

Unfortunately for Lithuanian workers and workers from the other nine new EU states, the prospect of a flood of workers from poor Eastern European nations was threatening to many of the richer nations of the EU. For example, many large European nations, like France and Germany, support large and expensive social welfare programs that give financial assistance, housing, and health care to their poor. The fear that waves of poor laborers will move in and drain the economies of these larger nations in millions of welfare dollars has caused most of the older EU countries to restrict the movement of labor to needed professionals.

Another segment of the Lithuanian population who may not benefit from EU accession are the nation's thousands of small farmers. Shortly after achieving independence, Lithuania implemented programs to privatize the country's large collective farms. Many young people, unhappy with factory work, took advantage of government incentives to relocate to rural areas and farm. Unfortunately, many of these farmers cannot meet the large **quotas** required to receive farm subsidies from the EU under its CAP program. As a result, these small farmers fear that they will lose local buyers for their products as produce from other EU nations makes its way to Lithuanian markets. These products will likely be less expensive than locally grown products due to the subsidies received by these larger farms in other areas of the EU. Only time will tell if these fears will be realized.

LOOKING FORWARD

While a few concerns over their sovereignty and national interests remain, there is little doubt that the EU will greatly improve the standard of living, economic security, and prominence of Lithuania on the world stage. The availability of EU funds for environmental cleanup, the development of a modern infrastructure and a favorable climate for foreign investment are helping to drive a steady recovery from the poverty that marked the nation's years as a communist state. The few drawbacks to Lithuanian membership in the EU are far outweighed by the potential benefits.

A Calendar of Lithuanian Festivals

Lithuania celebrates many important festivals and days of remembrance. These celebrations may be religious in nature, celebrate important dates relating to agriculture and the harvest, or commemorate an important event in Lithuanian history.

January: January 1 is a public holiday. The **New Year** festivities traditionally include champagne and fireworks. January 6, or **Three Kings Day**, is a celebration of the visit paid by the three wise men to the baby Jesus. This holiday marks the end of the holiday season and is usually celebrated with a parade. January 13 is **Independence Commemoration Day**. This date commemorates those killed or wounded by Soviet troops on January 13, 1991. Wreaths are placed on the pavement where partisans were killed. Lithuanians visit their graves, which are in one spot at the principal cemetery in Vilnius where most national heroes are buried. January 25 celebrates **Kirmeline**, or the Day of Serpents. This marks the traditional day when the serpents come out of the forests and return to the houses. On that day, the people would shake the fruit trees in the orchard so that they would be more fruitful and knock on beehives, waking the bees from their winter slumber.

February: Pusiauzemis, the midwinter festival is celebrated in early February. This celebration is a time of merrymaking since spring will soon arrive. Typically, women host a feast, feeding men a potent alcoholic brew of mushrooms and herbs. Watching the drunken men's behavior carefully, women then start searching out possible mates among the men. February 16 marks **Independence Day**, celebrating the initial independence of Lithuania in 1918.

March/April: Restoration of Independence Day is celebrated on March 11, marking the decision made in 1990 to sever ties with the Soviet Union and reinstate Lithuanian sovereignty. **Uzgavenes** is celebrated on Shrove Tuesday in early March and represents the last day before Lent. This celebration is full of humor, jokes, superstitions, fortune-telling, and feasting to celebrate the end of winter. It is a merry carnival, a masquerade full of pranks, with a drama performed outdoors to say goodbye to winter and welcome to spring. **Gavenes** or Lent is the forty-day abstinence from milk and meat observed by Lithuanian Catholics before Easter. Easter may fall in March or April, and the holiday is celebrated throughout the country.

June: June 23 and 24 are celebrated as **Midsummer's Eve** and **St. John's Festival**. These festivals date back to pagan times and celebrate the summer solstice. This celebration is always met with great joy as it marks the return of summer and its longer days. Celebrations revolve around nature's most powerful forces. Women adorn their heads with wreaths of flowers and leaves while the men opt for the more masculine oak leaf crowns. Fortune-telling and bonfires are also important elements of these festivities.

August: August 15 is **Zoline**, or Herb Day, an important holiday for honoring nature. Once a pagan festival, the celebration is now in honor of the Virgin Mary. In Lithuania, bouquets of flowers and ears of grain are brought to church to receive the blessings of the Virgin Mary. Lithuanians then continue the celebration with a great feast.

September: September 8 is **Nation Day**, which celebrates the freedom and independence of the modern Lithuanian State. **Baltic Unity Day** on September 22 celebrates the victory of united Latvian and Lithuanian forces against German crusaders in 1236.

November: Velines on November 2 is the Lithuanian Feast for the Dead. Traditionally, the holiday was a month long, culminating the first week of November. Today, under Christian influence, it has been reduced to one day. Lithuanians still celebrate Velines by visiting the graves of the recently deceased and those of long-departed family members.

December: Christmas festivities take place on December 24 and 25. Families gather for a traditional meatless feast on Christmas Eve, and a number of ancient customs are still observed at this important meal. After dinner children are expected to earn any presents they are to receive on Christmas by performing a song or dance or reciting a poem. Religious worship and a gift exchange are also traditional elements of a Lithuanian Christmas. **New Year's Eve** celebrations begin at nightfall on December 31, and often last well into the next morning.

Ausytes Su Grybais
(Little Mushroom Ears)

Ingredients
3 cups flour
2 eggs
2 cups chopped, raw mushrooms
1 medium onion, finely diced
2 tablespoons butter
2 tablespoons sour cream
salt and pepper
water

Directions
Make the mushroom filling first by sautéing the onion and combining with mushrooms, and one egg. Add salt and pepper to taste. Next prepare the dough by combining the flour and the second egg with a pinch of salt. Add water gradually until a dough about the consistency of pasta dough is achieved. Roll the dough out on a floured surface until thin and cut into two-inch squares. Place a drop of filling in the center of each square and fold into triangles, pinching the edges closed. Boil in salted water for about five minutes, then serve in a pan topped with melted butter and sour cream.

Kastinis

This is a traditional main dish and a staple of the Lithuanian diet.

Ingredients
1 pound butter
16 ounces sour cream
1 large chopped onion, sautéed
salt and pepper to taste

Directions
In a double boiler combine equal parts butter and sour cream one spoonful at a time. Continuously stir the mixture with a wooden spoon. When the ingredients have formed a thick mass in the bottom of the boiler pan add the onions and salt and pepper to taste. Pour into individual bowls and let cool, serve with rye bread and boiled potatoes.

Spanguoliu Kisielius
(Cranberry Pudding)

Ingredients
1 pound fresh cranberries
8 cups warm water
4 cups sugar
several cinnamon sticks
5 whole cloves
potato flour

Directions
Cover the cranberries with the warm water and bring to a gentle boil. When cranberries begin to break open, remove from heat. Smash the berries through a strainer, retaining the juice and pulp, and discard the leftover skin. For each cup of the pulp and juice mixture you will need 1 teaspoon of potato flour. Set aside a small amount of juice to dissolve the potato flour. In a saucepan combine the sugar with the juice and pulp, using half a cup of sugar for every two cups of juice. Add the cloves and cinnamon and bring to a gentle boil. Gradually add the potato flour, stirring constantly. Once the pudding has thickened and becomes clear, remove it from heat and pour into individual bowls. Let cool.

PROJECT AND REPORT IDEAS

Maps

- Make a map of the eurozone, and create a legend to indicate key manufacturing industries throughout the EU.
- Create a map of Lithuania using a legend to represent all the major products produced there. The map should clearly indicate all of the cities mentioned in this book.

Reports

- Write a brief report on Lithuania's cities.
- Many of Lithuania's industries today were centrally planned by Moscow during the communist era. Write a report discussing the advantages and disadvantages of this situation. How does it affect the products produced in Lithuania today?
- Write a report on Lithuania's concerns within the EU.
- Write a brief report on any of the following historical events: World War I, World War II, the movement for Lithuanian Independence.

Journal

- Imagine you are a student living in Latvia today. What things about your life have changed since independence, what things have stayed the same? Write a journal about your experience and discuss your feelings about your country's future.
- Read more about Lithuania's cities and culture. Plan a vacation in Lithuania and write a journal describing your travels and the places you visited.

Projects

- Learn the Lithuanian expressions for simple words such as hello, good day, please, and thank you. Try them on your friends.
- Make a calendar of your country's festivals and list the ones that are common or similar in Lithuania. Are they celebrated differently in Lithuania? If so, how?
- Go online or to the library and find images of medieval fortresses. Create a model of one.
- Make a protest poster for Lithuanian independence.
- Make a list of all the places that you have read about in this book and indicate them on a map of Lithuania.
- Find a Lithuanian recipe other than the ones given in this book, and ask an adult to help you make it. Share it with members of your class.

Group Activities

- Debate: One side should take the role of Germany and the other Lithuania. Germany's position is that EU should adopt a supranational approach, while Lithuania will speak in favor of the intergovernmental mode.
- Role play: Create and act out a peaceful protest against communist rule. Create posters and slogans that communicate your demands.

CHRONOLOGY

9000 BCE	Lithuania's earliest inhabitants arrive, after the withdrawal of the glaciers.
2000 BCE	Baltic tribes (ancestors of modern Lithuanians) first settle the territory.
900 CE	Baltic tribes form into separate cultural groups.
1230	The first Lithuanian state is established by King Mindaugas.
1386	Jagiello accepts the Polish crown and allies Lithuania with Poland. Lithuania converts to Roman Catholicism.
1569	The Polish-Lithuanian Commonwealth is established.
1795	Lithuania becomes a province of czarist Russia.
1850	The Lithuanian nationalist movement is born.
1914	World War I begins.
1918	Lithuania proclaims its independence.
1940	Soviet occupation of Lithuania begins.
1941	Nazi troops occupy Lithuania.
1945	Germany is defeated in World War II, and the Soviets begin to reinstate their occupation of Lithuania.
1989	Baltic States unite to peacefully protest communist rule.
1990	Newly elected parliament declares reinstatement of Lithuanian independence.
1991	Lithuanian independence is officially recognized.
2004	Lithuania joins NATO and the EU.

Further Reading/Internet resources

Iwaskiw, Walter, R. *Estonia, Latvia, and Lithuania: Country Studies*. Collingdale, Pa.: DIANE Publishing Company, 1997.

Kagda, Sakina. *Lithuania*. New York: Benchmark Books, 1997.

Kasubaite-Binder, Rima, and Elise S. Sheffield. *Destination: Lithuania*. Collingdale, Pa.: DIANE Publishing Company, 1995.

Lane, Thomas. *Lithuania: Stepping Westward*. New York: Routledge, 2002.

Smith, Graham, A. *Baltic States: The National Self-Determination of Estonia, Latvia, and Lithuania*. New York: St. Martin's Press, 1996.

Travel Information
www.lonelyplanet.com
www.visitlithuania.net

History and Geography
www.photius.com
www.workmall.com

Culture and Festivals
www.infoplease.com
www.lfcc.lt/kc/indexen.htm

Economic and Political Information
www.cia.gov/cia/publications/factbook
www.wikipedia.org

EU Information
europa.eu.int

FOR MORE INFORMATION

Embassy of Lithuania
2622 16th. Street, NW
Washington DC 20009
Tel.: 202-234-5860
Fax: 202-328-0466

Lithuanian State Department of Tourism
A. Juozapaviciaus 13
LT-09311 Vilnius, Lithuania
Tel.: 370-5-210-8796
Fax: 370-5210-8753

U.S. Embassy in Lithuania
2600 Akmenu 6
Vilnius, Lithuania
Tel.: 370-5-266-5500
Fax: 370-5-266-5510

European Union
Delegation of the European Commission to the United States
2300 M Street, NW
Washington DC 20037
Tel.: 202-862-9500
Fax: 202-429-1766

Glossary

activists: People who act vigorously and sometimes aggressively on behalf of a cause.

agrarian: Relating to farming or rural life.

annexed: Took over a territory and incorporated it into another political entity.

assimilated: Integrated someone into a larger group in a manner to minimize or eliminate differences.

augury: An indication of what will happen in the future.

authoritarian: Belonging to a political system in which obedience to the ruling person or group is strongly enforced.

autonomous: Self-governing.

blocs: United groups of countries.

capital: Wealth in the form of money or property.

capitalist: Practicing or supporting capitalism, an economic system based on the private ownership of the means of production and distribution of goods, and characterized by a free market and profit.

Catholicize: To influence someone or something to become Catholic.

censored: Restricted.

coalition government: A government formed by a temporary union between two or more groups.

compulsory: Required.

coup: The sudden overthrow of a government and seizure of political power.

czarist: Characteristic of absolute rule by anyone, especially the cruel abuse of power by a czar.

deportation: The banishment or expulsion of someone from his or her own country.

dissidents: Those who publicly disagree with an established political or religious system or organization.

dissonant: Making a combination of sounds that is unpleasant to listen to.

elite: A small group of people within a larger group who have more power, social standing, wealth, or talent than the rest of the group.

entrepreneurial: Having to do with the taking on of risk and benefits of running a business.

excise: A government-imposed tax on domestic goods.

fauna: A region's animal life.

flora: A region's plant life.

glasnost: A policy that commits a government or organization to greater accountability, openness, discussion, and freer disclosure of information.

gross domestic product (GDP): The total market value of all the goods and services produced by a nation during a specified period.

guerrilla: An irregular paramilitary unit, usually with some political objectives.

homogeneous: Having a uniform composition or structure.

immolated: Committed suicide as a form of protest, especially by burning.

information technology: The use of technologies such as computing and telecommunications to process and distribute information in digital and other forms.

infrastructure: A country's large-scale public systems, services, and facilities that are necessary for economic activity.

market economy: An economy in which most goods and services are produced and distributed through free markets rather than one based on government intervention.

nationalism: A strong sense of pride or devotion to a country.

nation-state: An independent country recognized by and able to interact with other such countries.

navigable: Deep and wide enough to accommodate ship or boat traffic.

neutral: Not belonging to any side in a conflict.

opportunists: Those who take advantage of a situation.

pagan: A follower of a polytheistic religion.

perestroika: The political and economic restructuring of the former Soviet Union by Mikhail Gorbachev beginning in 1986, characterized by decentralized control of industry and agriculture and allowing some private ownership.

polyphonic: Consisting of two or more independent melodic lines, parts, or voices that sound simultaneously.

power vacuum: A political condition in which no ruling authority exists.

privatization: The transfer to private ownership of economic enterprise or public utility that has been under state ownership.

progressive: Having to do with growth and development.

propaganda: Information put out by an organization or government to spread and promote a policy, idea, doctrine, or cause.

protectorate: A country or region that is defended and controlled by a more powerful nation.

puppet government: A government whose actions are controlled by others.

quotas: Maximum allowable quantities.

ratified: Officially approved.

referendum: A vote by the whole of an electorate on a specific question or questions put to it by a government.

Russification: To make Russian in character or quality; to give the characteristic of being from Russia.

service sector: The part of the economy that provides services rather than products.

solidarity: The act of standing together, presenting a united front.

sovereignty: Self-government free from outside interference.

stagnancy: A period of inactivity.

statehood: The status of being an independent nation.

subsidies: Government grants to a private company, organization, or charity to help it continue to function.

sustainable: Using the natural resources without destroying an area's ecological balance.

tariff: Tax levied by governments on goods, usually imports.

INDEX

PICTURE CREDITS

BIOGRAPHIES

AUTHOR

Heather Docalavich first developed an interest in the history and cultures of Eastern Europe through her work as a genealogy researcher. She currently resides in Hilton Head, South Carolina, with her four children.

SERIES CONSULTANTS

Ambassador John Bruton served as Irish Prime Minister from 1994 until 1997. As prime minister, he helped turn Ireland's economy into one of the fastest-growing in the world. He was also involved in the Northern Ireland Peace Process, which led to the 1998 Good Friday Agreement. During his tenure as Ireland's prime minister, he also presided over the European Union presidency in 1996 and helped finalize the Stability and Growth Pact, which governs management of the euro. Before being named the European Commission Head of Delegation in the United States, he was a member of the convention that drafted the European Constitution, signed October 29, 2004.

The European Commission Delegation to the United States represents the interests of the European Union as a whole, much as ambassadors represent their countries' interests to the U.S. government. Matters coming under European Commission authority are negotiated between the commission and the U.S. administration.